What are you scared of?

Hanne Larsen

Photographs by
Eric Larsen

Adam & Charles Black·London

Larsen, Hanne
    What are you scared of?
    1. Fear (Child psychology)—Juvenile
    literature
    I. Title
    155.4   BF723.F4
    ISBN 0-7136-1917-1

A & C Black (Publishers) Limited
35 Bedford Row, London WC1R 4JH
© 1979 (English text) A & C Black Limited
© 1977 Hanne Larsen
ISBN 0 7136 1917 1
Translated from Danish by Bente Jacobsen.
First published in this edition 1979.
Originally published by Borgens Forlag, Copenhagen, with
the title *Hvad er du bange for?*

Printed in Great Britain by W S Cowell Ltd., Ipswich

I'm afraid of deep water. I like playing on the beach though. It's fun to make sandcastles and to sit at the edge of the water digging harbours and things like that.

But I don't like to go out into the deep water. Once my dad took me there, and even though he held on to me I was really frightened.

I held on to his neck very tightly and cried because it was so cold and I couldn't touch the bottom.

My dad turned back at once and said I would probably be more daring next year. Then he ran out again on his own, and I went on playing at the edge of the water. Do you like deep water?

I'm afraid of walking on my own in the dark.

Sometimes it seems as if someone is following me, and
I run as fast as I can to a place where there is somebody I know or where it is light, and slam the door after me. And then it's nice if I can hold someone's hand afterwards.

I've got a light next to my bed so that I can turn it on if I have to go for a pee in the night. If I have to go outside when it's dark I switch on the light and leave the door open so that I can hear the others in the sitting-room, and then I'm not so scared.

Are you afraid of the dark?

I'm scared if I meet a dog.

If it's on a lead, I keep as far away as I can so that it can't get me. But if it's on its own I get scared stiff and can't move.

When the dog has gone I run home and cry.

When my mum or dad holds my hand I'm not all that frightened – sometimes I even feel like patting the dog. But my mum and dad say I shouldn't pat dogs I don't know because you never know whether they'll bite or not.

Are you afraid of dogs?

Sometimes I'm afraid of big children I don't know.

I'm afraid they will tease or hit me. When I have to pass a big boy I don't know, my heart starts thumping, and I try not to look at him.

When I have passed him I start half walking, half running so that he can't see I'm afraid, and so that I can get away quickly.

Are you scared of children you don't know?

I tried a big wheel once. I was really scared. When I was looking at it from below I thought it seemed fun, and it didn't look too high.

But when I was up there and it started turning round, I got really scared. There were some other people on the seat – they laughed and swung the chair.

I didn't dare say anything at all, I just held on tight.

I'm never going on a thing like that again, and I don't like going on the switchback either – do you?

I'm afraid of going to the dentist. When I sit in the dentist's chair I get tummy ache. When the dentist looks in my mouth I can hear my heart thumping.

It's a really good feeling when he says there are no holes and I can go without having my teeth drilled.

Sometimes the lady at the dentist's gives me a tooth-brush. I use it every day so that I don't get any holes.

Are you afraid of going to the dentist?

I get very frightened when my mum and dad quarrel.

I don't like it when they shout or are rude to each other. I cry and try to make them stop.

Sometimes I hide in my bed and pull the eiderdown over my head so that I can't hear anything.

When my mum and dad have made it up, we are very happy. Then I am glad I've got such nice parents.

Are you unhappy when your mum and dad quarrel?

I'm scared when there's a storm. When there's lightning I hide by my mum or dad. I cuddle up to them so that I can't see it and cover my ears with a cushion so that I don't hear the thunder, but I still can't stop myself from listening.

I tried to sit by the window with my mum and dad and look at the lightning.

But that was while the thunder was so far away that I couldn't hear it. All of a sudden I heard it – my tummy started turning over and I started to cry. I was so frightened that the lightning would hit our house.

Are you afraid of storms?

I got lost once. All of a sudden my mum wasn't there. I went round looking for her and calling her but I couldn't see her. I got frightened – perhaps she'd forgotten all about me and gone home.

Then I started to cry. A woman came up and asked me what was wrong. I've lost my mother, I said. She said she would help me find her.

We went up to some other women who asked me my name and address. Then one of them called my mother over the loud-speaker and said I was waiting for her.

When I saw my mum coming to get me I started crying again. My mum lifted me up and said she'd been frightened too, and she was glad she had found me.

I'm afraid of a man who looks strange.

Down my road there's a man who limps. He's got a walking stick and wears a big coat and hat. Some of the other children say he's a wicked old man.

When he comes walking along the street we run into a doorway at the foot of a staircase and hide until he has passed.

I get so frightened that he will follow us.

I've told my mum but she says he's just an ordinary man with a bad leg. I'm still afraid of him though.

Are you frightened of people who look strange?

I'm scared to cross the road on my own.

My mum and dad have told me how dangerous it is, and when I try to cross there are always cars.

Even though they are right at the other end of the street, they drive so fast that I haven't got time to cross.

When Mum is with me she holds my hand and we always use the zebra crossing. Even then I'm afraid when a car is coming. What if the driver hasn't seen us and runs us over! I always hold my mum's hand very tightly.

Do you know how to cross the road?

I don't like being alone in the house in the evening.

I lie still and listen hard to see if somebody is there. I can't get to sleep.

When I've been lying there for a long time looking into the dark I start to get scared – I imagine there's somebody in the house and I get more and more frightened.

Suddenly I hear slight noises at the front door – it opens, the light is switched on and I hear talking. My mum and dad have come back.

When they come in to see me, I pretend I'm asleep. I feel nice and warm, and I'm really tired.

Do you like being alone in the house?

I'm really scared that there will be a war here.

My dad says 'probably not', but when I watch television I am afraid if there is shooting and pictures of dead people.

Sometimes there are bombs left in shopping centres.

When I go to bed I wonder what would happen if it had been my mum and dad who had been shot or got blown up by a bomb – what would I do then?

Do you like watching war on television?

I'm afraid of heights. Once I was taken up into a very tall building – a block of flats.

First we went in the lift. That gave me butterflies in my tummy and I was a bit afraid. Then we had to go up some steps, and then we got to the door leading to the roof. You could see the whole town from there. I went to the edge and looked down.

I got really scared! I thought I would fall down even though there was a guard rail all the way round. The people and the cars were very small. I stopped looking at once and sat down. Then I crawled so far back I couldn't look down any more. When I got up my legs were shaking and I felt strange.

Do you like heights?

Sometimes I'm afraid that my mum and dad don't love me any more.

When I've done something I'm not supposed to, my parents tell me off and I don't think they love me at all.

Sometimes they even say that I'll be sent away if I don't behave. That's when I feel afraid and sad.

Do your mum and dad ever get angry with you?

I'm afraid to admit that I'm afraid. I think that there might be people who will laugh at me and then I would be ashamed.

There are also some grown-ups who say it's silly to be afraid of something or other.

Aren't grown-ups ever afraid of anything then?

Sometimes I boast to show that I'm not afraid – but I still am.

Isn't there something you are afraid of?

Once I was down in the basement with some of the big boys. One of them had brought cigarettes that they were going to smoke.

They said I had to smoke one too. At first I didn't want to because I didn't dare. Then they said that I was a little sissy and that I could clear off because I didn't even dare smoke a fag.

I took one because if not I wouldn't have anybody to play with.

It tasted awful and I got smoke in my eyes – that hurt. It made me cough and I dropped the cigarette. The others laughed at me and one of them finished it.

Have you ever tried doing something you didn't want to do?

I tried to light a match by myself. I didn't like it because I was afraid of burning myself. I got so scared when the match was alight that I threw the match and the box on the floor. It lay there burning and I was really frightened that the house would catch fire, but my mum stepped on it and it went out.

Mum has helped me light matches lots of times.

She holds the box and she also holds my hand with the match in it. She says that I should strike it away from myself. I'm not so frightened then, but I still shake a little.

My mum also says I'm only allowed to try striking matches when there are grown-ups around because it can be dangerous. Are you scared of fire?